Our Guests

Cover Image by D. Morgan

HARVEST HOUSE PUBLISHERS

EUGENE, OREGON

Morgan Guest Book

Copyright © 2005 by Harvest House Publishers
Eugene, Oregon 97402

ISBN-13: 978-0-7369-1624-0
ISBN-10: 0-7369-1624-5

Cover art is copyrighted by D. Morgan and licensed by Grace Licensing, Bainbridge, IN and may not be copied or reproduced without permission. For more information, please contact:

> Grace Licensing
> 7796 North CR 100 East
> Bainbridge, IN 46105
> (877) 210-3456

Cover by Koechel Peterson & Associates, Minneapolis, Minnesota

Harvest House Publishers has made every effort to trace the ownership of all poems and quotes. In the event of a question arising from the use of a poem or quote, we regret any error made and will be pleased to make the necessary correction in future editions of this book.

Scripture quotations are taken from *The Living Bible,* Copyright ©1971. Used by permission of Tyndale House Publishers, Inc., Wheaton, IL 60189 USA. All rights reserved.

Printed in China

05 06 07 08 09 10 11 12 13 / LP / 10 9 8 7 6 5 4 3 2 1

Blest be that spot, where cheerful guests retire
To pause from toil, and trim their ev'ning fire;
Blest that abode, where want and pain repair,
And every stranger finds a ready chair.

OLIVER GOLDSMITH

Date   *Guests*

Date   *Guests*

Date   *Guests*

Date   *Guests*

Date   Guests

Date   *Guests*

Date   Guests

Date   Guests

His house was perfect,
whether you liked food, or sleep,
or work, or story-telling, or singing,
or just sitting and thinking best,
or a pleasant mix of them all.

J.R.R. TOLKIEN

Date   Guests

Date   Guests

Date   *Guests*

Date　　　Guests

Date   Guests

Date   Guests

Date   Guests

Date   *Guests*

_____ _____

_____ _____

_____ _____

_____ _____

_____ _____

_____ _____

_____ _____

_____ _____

_____ _____

_____ _____

_____ _____

$\mathcal{D}$ate $\mathcal{G}$uests

*Cheerfully share your home
with those who need a meal
or a place to stay for the night.*

THE BOOK OF 1 PETER

Date   *Guests*

Date   Guests

Date   *Guests*

Date   *Guests*

Date   Guests

Date   *Guests*

No matter where I travel
Or just how far I roam…
There's just no other place
Quite as nice as home.

D. MORGAN

Date　　　Guests

Date   Guests

Date   Guests

Date   Guests

Date   Guests

Date   Guests

Date   Guests

Date   *Guests*

Date   _Guests_

My home is a treasure chest,
in which I collect memories of my family and friends.

CLARA FERREE-SMITH

Date   *Guests*

Date   *Guests*

Date   Guests

Date   Guests

Date   *Guests*

Date   *Guests*

There's a little bit of heaven—
'Round the corner, take a right
A cozy little cottage
With a little kitchen light…
A comfort when I'm weary
A refuge when I'm blue
There's a little bit of heaven
Here at home with you.

D. MORGAN

Date　　　Guests

Date   Guests

Date   Guests

Date   *Guests*

Date   *Guests*

Date   *Guests*

Date   *Guests*

Date   Guests

Date	Guests

*Homes really are no more
than the people who live in them.*

NANCY REAGAN

Date   *Guests*

Date   *Guests*

Date   Guests

Date   Guests

Date   Guests

Date   Guests

If my dreams could all come true
Paradise would be
In a little bungalow
Somewhere by the sea…

D. Morgan

Date　　　Guests

Date   Guests

Date   Guests

Date   *Guests*

Date   Guests

Date　　　Guests

Date   *Guests*

Date   *Guests*

Date   *Guests*

May this home be full of love
With His richest blessings from above
From morning sun to evening prayer
We count on Him…He's always there.

D. MORGAN

Date   *Guests*

Date   Guests

Date   Guests

Date   Guests

Date   Guests

Date   *Guests*

Under our thatch, friend,
Place shall abide for you,
Touch but the latch, friend,
The door will swing wide for you!

NANCY BYRD TURNE

Date   Guests

Date   Guests

Date Guests

Date Guests

Date　　　Guests

Date　　Guests

Date   *Guests*

Date   *Guests*

Date   Guests

Date　　　　Guests

Date   *Guests*

Date   Guests

Date   Guests

Date   Guests

Date   Guests

Date   *Guests*

Date   Guests

Date   *Guests*

Date   Guests

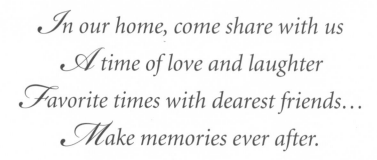

In our home, come share with us
A time of love and laughter
Favorite times with dearest friends…
Make memories ever after.

D. MORGAN